Amazing Animals
Giant Pandas

Don Cruickshank

WEIGL PUBLISHERS INC.

Published by Weigl Publishers Inc.
350 5th Avenue, Suite 3304
New York, NY USA 10118-0069

Library of Congress Cataloging-in-Publication
Data

Cruickshank, Don, 1977-
  Giant pandas / Don Cruickshank.
    p. cm. – (Amazing animals series)
  ISBN 1-59036-389-2 (hard cover : alk. paper)
  – ISBN 1-59036-395-7 (soft cover : alk. paper)
  1. Giant panda–Juvenile literature. I. Title. II.
Series.
  QL737.C214C78 2006
  599.789–dc22

                                    2005027263

Printed in the United States of America
1 2 3 4 5 6 7 8 9 0 10 09 08 07 06

COVER: A giant panda's cute and cuddly
features make it a favorite animal for many
people around the world.

Editor
Heather C. Hudak
Design and Layout
Terry Paulhus

About This Book

This book tells you all about giant
pandas. Find out where they live
and what they eat. Discover how
you can help to protect them. You
can also read about them in myths
and legends from around
the world.

Words in **bold** are explained in the
Words to Know section at the back
of the book.

Useful Websites

Addresses in this book
take you to the home pages
of websites that have information
about giant pandas.

All of the Internet URLs given in the
book were valid at the time of
publication. However, due to the
dynamic nature of the Internet, some
addresses may have changed, or sites
may have ceased to exist since
publication. While the author and
publisher regret any inconvenience this
may cause readers, no responsibility
for any such changes can be accepted
by either the author or the publisher.

Contents

Meet the Giant Panda

Giant pandas look cute and cuddly. Their adorable features make them a very popular animal with people around the world. Giant pandas live in the mountains and forests in China.

▼ Giant pandas spend most of their time finding and eating bamboo.

Giant pandas are **mammals**. Like other mammals, the young drink their mother's milk.

Useful Websites

www.sandiegozoo.org/zoo/ ex__panda__station.html

Search giant pandas at this website to learn more about this amazing animal.

The Amazing Giant Panda

- Giant pandas are flexible. They can touch their heads with their hind feet.

- Giant pandas can make 12 different sounds.

- Giant pandas can live up to 20 years in the wild.

▲ Humans rarely see giant pandas in nature because they are shy animals.

A Very Special Animal

Giant pandas spend most of their time looking for bamboo. This kind of grass is difficult to chew. Giant pandas have razor-sharp teeth and extremely powerful jaws that are perfect for chewing.

Giant pandas have an **opposable thumb**. This thumb helps them to grip the bamboo stalks while they eat. Without these special features, giant pandas would have a difficult time eating bamboo.

▶ Giant pandas have large cheek muscles to help them chew bamboo.

Black around a panda's eyes make the eyes look bigger than they are.

Strong claws and a firm grip help pandas climb trees easily.

Razor-sharp teeth and strong jaws are useful for eating bamboo.

Black fur keeps pandas warm by keeping heat in.

White fur cools giant pandas by keeping heat out.

Black and white fur serves as **camouflage**.

7

Living Alone

Giant pandas usually live alone. They rarely come into conflict with one another. In panda **habitats**, bamboo is usually so plentiful that the bears do not have to fight over food.

Giant pandas are **territorial**. They leave their scent marks on objects in their environment. These markings warn other pandas of their presence.

During mating season, giant pandas spend most of their time finding a mate. They are most active at this time.

▶ Giant pandas rarely leave their own territory.

Daily Activities

Giant pandas are active animals.

- Giant pandas are mainly land animals. They are found in trees where there is plenty of bamboo to eat.

- Giant pandas take shelter in hollow fir trees and thick bush.

- During the day, giant pandas rest, eat, and search for food. They are more active at night.

▲ In the winter, giant pandas move from the mountains to lower land where it is warmer.

How Giant Pandas Eat

About 99 percent of a giant panda's diet is made up of bamboo. They will eat meat from dead animals if it is available. Giant pandas will also eat wild parsnip, horsetails, willow leaves, and bark from fir trees.

Giant pandas eat sitting up or lying on their backs. This position helps free all their paws to eat bamboo. They eat the softer **fibers** inside bamboo stalks. Giant pandas can peel and eat a bamboo shoot in less than a minute.

▼ Giant pandas have a special lining in their throat to protect it from bamboo splinters.

A Big Appetite

- On average, giant pandas eat between 25 and 30 pounds (11 and 14 kilograms) of bamboo every day.

- In the spring, they will eat up to 100 pounds (45 kg) of bamboo each day.

- Giant pandas usually eat for 8 hours, sleep for 4 hours, and then start eating again.

▲ Giant pandas eat large amounts of bamboo to get enough nutrients for their bodies.

Where Do They Live?

Fossil records show that giant pandas once lived in many different places in China. Today, they only live in the mountains and wet forests of southwestern China. Giant pandas are found in the provinces of Sichuan, Gansu, and Shaanxi. They live in these areas because bamboo grows plentifully there.

Useful Websites

http://nationalzoo.si.edu

Click on the giant panda icon to learn more about where they live.

▶ Giant pandas are found in misty bamboo forests high in the mountains of China.

Giant Panda Range

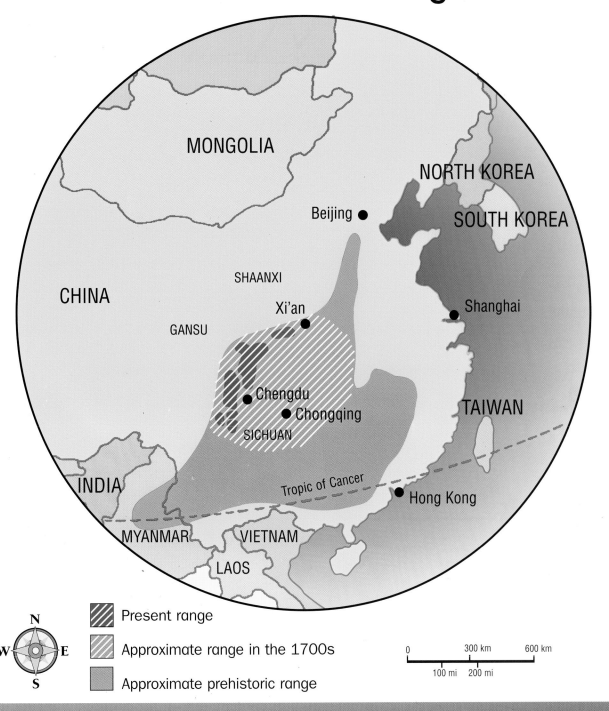

Present range

Approximate range in the 1700s

Approximate prehistoric range

Friends and Enemies

Giant pandas peacefully share the bamboo forests with many other animals. These animals include red pandas, bamboo rats, and other giant pandas.

Giant pandas spend much of their time looking for food. They rarely come into conflict with other animals or other giant pandas. Giant pandas will compete with red pandas and bamboo rats when there is not enough bamboo to eat.

▼ Giant pandas communicate with each other by bleating. This sound is like a gentle cry.

Useful Websites

www.encarta.com

Search giant pandas at this website to learn more about animal life in China.

Leopards sometimes attack giant pandas. Weasels, martens, and wild dogs hunt panda cubs.

Human activities are a threat to giant pandas. Hunting, pollution, and habitat loss have led to a decline in the population of giant pandas.

▶ Giant pandas lead a simple and peaceful existence.

Growing Up

Giant panda cubs are usually born in August or September. At birth, they are pink and very tiny, weighing just over 2 ounces (56 grams). Newborn panda cubs can fit in the palm of a human hand.

The first month of a giant panda cub's life is spent cradled in its mother's arms. The mother carries her cub in her mouth when traveling. At night, the mother sleeps sitting up, with her cub held carefully in her arms.

▶ A giant panda mother is about 900 times larger than her newborn cub.

Growth Chart

1 to 4 weeks	2 to 5 ounces (57 to 142 g)	A newborn giant panda is tiny, pink, blind, and toothless. After one week, a giant panda cub starts to grow black-and-white fur.
5 to 11 weeks	7 pounds (3 kilograms)	At 6 weeks, cubs open their eyes. They move around by wriggling or rolling side to side.
12 to 28 weeks	22 pounds (10 kg)	Cubs learn how to stand and walk. They develop climbing skills.
29 to 52 weeks	45 pounds (5 kg)	Cubs learn how to communicate.
5 or 6 years old	200 to 265 pounds (90 to 120 kg)	Giant pandas are full grown and ready to mate.

▼ The mother plays with her cubs by rolling and wrestling with them.

Under Threat

There are about 1,000 giant pandas left in the world. Some giant pandas live in city zoos. Giant pandas are an **endangered species**.

In 1939, the government of China created a law to protect giant pandas from hunters. Still, humans continue to hunt giant pandas for their **pelts**. Habitat loss is a serious threat to the giant panda population. The growth of farms and villages make it difficult for pandas to find food. Giant pandas now face **extinction**.

▼ More than 160 giant pandas live in city zoos and breeding centers.

What Do You Think?

Some people think that zoos will help save the panda population. The problem is that some panda parents taken from forests never breed in **captivity**. Should giant pandas be put in zoos for breeding programs? Should giant pandas remain in their natural habitat?

▲ Giant pandas are now so rare that zoos may be the only way to help them survive in China.

Myths and Legends

Giant pandas are national treasures in China. Today, giant pandas are popular subjects in Chinese artwork and stories.

Black Markings

Four young girls were walking in the forests in China. They saw a leopard attacking a giant panda. The girls tried to help the giant panda, but were killed in the process. The other giant pandas held a funeral to honor the bravery of these innocent girls.

▼ Giant pandas are a symbol of peace in China.

At the funeral, the giant pandas wore black arm bands. They cried so hard that their arm bands began to leak black dye. When they held their ears and rubbed their eyes, their ears and eyes turned black. When they hugged each other, their bodies were blackened. This is how giant pandas got their black markings.

▶ Giant pandas are welcomed as guests if they wander into villages in China.

Quiz

1. Where do giant pandas live?
(a) **bamboo forests** (b) **deserts** (c) **swamps**

2. What do giant pandas eat most?
(a) **fish** (b) **bananas** (c) **bamboo**

3. What time of day are giant pandas more active?
(a) **afternoon** (b) **morning** (c) **night**

4. What animals may attack a giant panda?
(a) **wild horses** (b) **leopards** (c) **monkeys**

5. What is a baby giant panda called?
(a) **pup** (b) **cub** (c) **calf**

Answers:
1. (a) Giant pandas live in bamboo forests.
2. (c) Giant pandas mostly eat bamboo.
3. (c) Giant pandas are more active at night.
4. (b) Leopards attack giant pandas.
5. (b) Baby giant pandas are called cubs.

22

Find out More

If you would like to find out more about giant pandas, visit the websites in this book. You can also write to the following organizations.

Pandas International
P.O. Box 620335
Littleton, CO 80123

World Wildlife Fund
1250 24th Street NW
Washington, DC 20037

American Zoo and Aquarium Association
8403 Colesville Road, Suite 710
Silver Spring, MD 20910-3314

Words to Know

camouflage
a feature an animal has to help it hide in its environment

captivity
the state of being confined

endangered species
at risk of no longer living on Earth

extinction
no longer living on Earth

fibers
threadlike plant tissues

habitats
the natural environments in which animals and plants live

mammals
animals that have hair or fur and feed milk to their young

opposable thumb
the ability to place the first finger and thumb together to grasp things

pelts
the hides of animals including their fur

territorial
the instinct an animal has to protect the area in which it lives

Index